HAKUIN'S SONG IN PRAISE OF

ZAZEN:

TEXT, ANALYSIS, AND

COMMENTARY

Dr. Frank Bryce McCluskey

ISBN-13: 9781795504560

DEDICATION

Kyudo Nakagawa

Sensei of the Soho Zen Buddhist Society

Sensei of the London Zen Society

Abbot of Ryutaku-ji

February 12, 1927—December 29, 2007

CONTENTS

FORWARD

This little work is my attempt to clarify Hakuin Zenzi's **Song in Praise of Zazen** for a friend. A fellow member of the Southern Palm Zen Group asked me if there was printed book I could suggest to help him understand The Song in Praise of Zazen that we chant as a group each week. I could not find any book that would answer his question. There was an excellent short work published in Japan in 1967 by Zenkei Shibayama on this subject but it is, sadly, out of print. There is an excellent book by Albert Lowe but only in digital form. Thus, here is this little work which I humbly present to you.

I am not a Zen Master or Sensei but a simple student and practitioner of Zen Buddhism. I am not a spokesperson for any school or tradition. I claim no authority or expertise except for my own study and practice of more than fifty years. These thoughts are my own and any errors contained in this text are mine and mine alone. Zen cannot be put into words. That said, I hope this little work is of some use to you. If you are a seasoned student of Zen you may want to skip the history of Buddhism and go to the analysis of the Song of Zazen.

The text used here is that chanted by some Sanghas of the White Plum Tradition. Thanks to Ms. Melanie Winter and Dr. Tom Collins for editorial assistance and spiritual guidance.

Hakuin's Song in Praise of Zazen

From the beginning all beings are Buddha (1)

Like water and ice, without water no ice

Outside us no Buddhas

How near the truth, yet how far we seek

Like one in water crying I thirst (5)

Like a son of rich birth, wandering poor on this earth.

We endlessly circle the six worlds

The cause of our sorrow is ego delusion

From dark path to dark path we've wandered in darkness.

How can we be free from birth and death? (10)

The gateway to freedom is Zazen samadhi

Beyond exaltation, beyond all our praises, the pure Mahayana

Observing the Precepts, Repentance and Giving,

the countless good deeds and the way of right living, all come from

zazen.

Thus one true samadhi extinguishes evils. It purifies karma,

dissolving obstructions. (15)

Then where are the dark paths to lead us astray?

The Pure Lotus Land is not far away.

Hearing this truth, heart humble and grateful.

To praise and embrace it, to practice its wisdom,

brings unending blessings. bring mountains of merit. (20)

And if we turn inward and prove our True Nature, that

True Self is no-self, our own self is no-self,

we go beyond ego and past clever words.

Then the gate to the oneness of cause-and-effect is thrown open.

Not two and not three, straight ahead runs the Way. (25)

Our form now being no-form,

in going and returning we never leave home.

Our thought now being no-thought,

our dancing and songs are the Voice of the Dharma.

How vast is the heaven of boundless Samadhi! (30)

How bright and transparent the moonlight of wisdom!

What is there outside us? What is there we lack?

Nirvana is openly shown to our eyes.

This land where we stand is the Pure Lotus Land

And this body, the Body of Buddha (35)

PART I: THE HISTORICAL CONTEXT

The Zazen Wasan or the Song in Praise of Zazen by Hakuin
Ekaku is a thing of wonder.   It is only 35 lines or 295 English
words in length (by my calculation) and can be chanted in less
than two minutes. Yet in this short song, Zen Master Hakuin has
conveyed the essence of Zen.   This is why it is a mainstay in
many Zen Buddhist temples.   It was written more than 250 years
ago and has withstood the test of time.   In this short little piece is
contained the wisdom of the ages and all of the essential teachings
of Mahayana Buddhism. The Song in Praise of Zazen was written
in Japanese for the common folk and not in the Chinese text that so
many scholars worked in during the time it was written.   In other
words, it is all of the esoteric wisdom of Buddhism in a language
almost anyone can understand.   It is a guide to liberation for the
common person. The Song in Praise of Zazen was not written for

monks or enlightened arhats, it was written for you and me.

A Short History of Buddhism

Let us place the Song in Praise of Zazen in its historical context. To do this we will go over a short history of Buddhism from its founder to the writing of The Song in Praise of Zazen. Buddhism is over two thousand years old. It was founded by a man whose full name was Siddhartha Gautama Shakyamuni Buddha who is now known by his title "the Buddha". In the ancient languages of his time, the word "Buddha" simply means to "wake up" or be awake. Siddhartha was born a prince who lived in luxury. But eventually he realized that we are all subject to change and when our situation changes that can make us suffer. If I am young, one day I will be old. When I am healthy, I realize one day I will die. If there is someone or something that is very dear to me, the time will come when I must leave them or they will leave me. These changes cause many of us pain. So the Buddha sought a way to escape the pain that change often brings. Buddha did not mean that ALL is suffering. That is obviously counter intuitive. There are many moments in life when we don't suffer. When I am enjoying food, watching a sunset, or meeting an old friend I am not suffering. Buddha only noticed that the same things that bring us joy by our possession of them can bring us pain by their loss.

So Buddha abandoned his wealth, his high station and his family and set out to see if there was an answer to the question "Can we free ourselves from suffering?". In other words, can we be at peace amidst all the changes and challenges of life? At first Buddha sought to escape from the world by denying it. He joined a group of strict religious men who believed that by punishing the flesh you can free the spirit. They denied themselves food and drink and led an ascetic religious life. But as we all know, that does not work. If I ask you now not to think of a yellow daffodil against a blue background, you know what happens. If I add that is it a sin to think about a yellow daffodil against a blue background that makes it worse. We are in the world and we can't escape from it, no matter how much mental and spiritual energy we expend trying to get away. After years of trying to escape change and suffering, the Buddha was exhausted and decided to sit cross legged under a bodhi tree until he figured it out. He sat in deep meditation for 49 days and as dawn rose one morning he saw the evening star and at that moment he felt himself freed from anxiety, resistance, frustration, and anger. At that moment, when his eyes were looking up at the sky, he placed one hand flat on the earth to show that while he woke up and was free, he was still firmly rooted on the earth and in the here and now. He understood that what he had been missing had been directly under his nose the whole time. In one sentence he was able to sum up what he grasped in that moment of realization. Reportedly, the sentence something like the following;

"Wonder of wonders! All living beings are Buddha, enlightened and compassionate, but we are too deluded to see this."

This is called Buddha's enlightenment statement. For me, this is the heart of Buddhist teaching, the kernel around which everything else is built. Those nineteen words are the foundation of everything that followed for 2,500 years. We will see when we get to The Song in Praise of Zazen, that the opening line is "From the very beginning, all beings are Buddha." This is a restatement of Buddha's first insight. We will see that the final line of the song, line 35, says "this very body is the body of Buddha." which takes Buddha's enlightenment statement and instead of applying it to all beings applies it the very person who is chanting The Song in Praise of Zazen. We will see that the first line and the last line are similar with the change going from "all beings" to "me here and now". In philosophical terms this is called the relation of the Universal and the Particular.

Buddha meditated for while and enjoyed his freedom but shortly realized that he had an obligation to teach others what he had learned. He spent the next 45 years of life teaching. The collection of these teachings have come to be called "the Dharma". If one were to read the teachings of Buddha, you would find simple instructions on how to free yourself from what Buddha called the "three poisons": greed, anger and ignorance. Once you free yourself from these three poisons, you also rid yourself of the anxieties, fears and regrets that govern so much of our lives. Buddha's ideas here echo to the teachings of the ancient Greek philosopher Socrates. Socrates is famous for his "Socratic Ignorance". This is his claim that the only thing he knows is that he knows nothing. At the same time the Oracle of Delphi, who was honored by the Greeks for her gift of prophecy, once said Socrates was the wisest of men. His wisdom was in not talking about things he didn't know. Buddha taught in the same spirit. Pay attention to the here and now. Don't focus your eyes on an afterlife or foreign lands or the shenanigans of politicians and movie stars. Taste your tea, watch the clouds go by and work to change yourself and by doing that you will help all beings achieve liberation. When it comes to changing the world we can sum up the Buddha's message as advice to focus on fixing ourselves before we take on the world. Rather than solving the problem of planetary war, I can ask myself how can I be less angry. Rather than railing against news or television coverage, I can ask myself how much do I gossip or talk ill of others. Buddha asks us to look inward and the Song in Praise of Zazen will teach us how to do this.

Buddha kept it simple, like Jesus. But years after both of them died, their followers began to embellish, add, and interpret. Jesus, who slept under the stars and said "the poor shall inherit the earth", eventually was seen as the inspiration for the Crusades, the Holy Roman Empire, the Inquisition, and the treasures of the Vatican. The same thing happened to Buddha. There are books on Buddhist logic, theories about the six worlds, and prayers to hungry ghosts. There are thousands of Buddhist gods and demigods people pray to and look to for guidance. There arose charms, spells, magic, and martial arts. There evolved a complicated hierarchy of priests, nuns, and monks. There arose experts in Buddhism and they created systems and rules that were very, very complicated. If Buddha were alive to see this, I believe that he would surely scratch his head in amazement.

Growing up in close proximity to Hinduism in India, Buddhism, after the death of the Buddha, entered a period of scholarship and intellectual complexity. As it spread to Tibet and Southeast Asia it transmuted into various schools with subtle differences. The schools battled each other and there conflicts arose about who was carrying on the authentic teachings of Buddha. But on our journey to understand The Song in Praise of Zazen we next meet a monk named Bodhidharma who brought it back to the simplicity it began with. Before we meet him we must first see what it means to be a teacher in the Buddhist tradition.

Buddha didn't teach people to pray, he wanted them instead to look inside themselves. Instead of writing things down, the teaching was done in person, from teacher to student. This made the role of the teacher critical. To make sure the next generation of teachers had the right insight, the Buddha began a tradition called "oral transmission" or "mind to mind transmission". This means that when a teacher recognizes that a student has understood the teachings of Buddhism called the Dharma, the teacher can recognize that student as a fellow teacher. This places the new teacher in a line of succession guaranteeing the spirit of the original teaching is unbroken. Thus, the line of teachers goes unbroken from the Buddha to our present-day teachers. My own teachers have been in this direct line of succession.

An important teacher in the history of Zen is the monk called the Bodhidharma who brought Buddhism from India to China. The Bodhidharma, who was separated from the Buddha by 28 generations of teachers, lived hundreds of years after the Buddha. In some accounts he is from India and in other accounts he said to be from Persia. In some accounts he had blue eyes, and in others a red beard. One legend tells us that because Buddhism had fallen into superstition and ritual, he left his home and journeyed East to China to spread Buddhism. Through the mists of history and legend, it is said he arrived in China during either the Liu Song dynasty (420-479) or the Liang dynasty (502-557).

In China, the Bodhidharma found a fertile field for the teachings of Buddha. The way was made easy because of the Taoist teachings of Lao Tzu and Chuang Tzu. Taoism was already well established in China when the Bodhidharma arrived. The Taoists taught that there was a force in the universe that they called the Tao. It flows through everything, living or not. It binds us all together and is never obstructed. The Taoists use the metaphor of water as something that flows until it meets an obstruction, then it simply finds a way to go around it. Its goal is to reach the lowest point and from the highest mountains on earth, water knows how to find its way to the sea. Later we will see the role water plays in The Song in Praise of Zazen.

Bodhidharma brought the line of transmission to China, of which he was 28th in the Indian line, and his Chinese followers began their own line of succession beginning with the First Chinese Patriarch. The school of Chinese Buddhism that traces itself back to the Bodhidharma is called Chan or Ch'an Buddhism. Chan is the Chinese word for meditation. This is a translation of the Sanskrit word Dhyana. When the same word is translated into Japanese it is called Zen. So the term Zen Buddhism literally translates into English as Meditation Buddhism. It is called Meditation Buddhism because it not about believing in a book, or a god, or a doctrine. The essence of Zen is meditation, pure and simple. There are many ways to meditate. Yoga is a kind of meditation. Tai Chi is sometimes called moving meditation. The heart of Zen Buddhism is Zazen or "sitting meditation". Za is a Japanese word which means to sit and Zen in the Japanese means to meditate. Whenever you sit in meditation or keep still as you meditate you are doing Zazen. It is my personal opinion that what we call Zen (not the full tradition of Zen Buddhism) is at the heart of all religions. Zen is keeping still, calming the mind, and listening in silence. The mystical traditions of all the religions of the world have practitioners (often called saints, arhats, or mystics) who have achieved this calmness of spirit and openness of mind.

The line in China established by the Bodhidharma began a new system of counting generations of authenticated teachers. We now start with the Second and Third Patriarch of the Chinese Buddhist tradition. Chan Buddhism took root in China and developed a long and storied tradition which is still alive there today. Because Chinese philosophy has always been about family and community, there developed doctrines about not just liberating yourself from suffering but liberating all beings. In Buddhism we don't separate people from all beings. Other religions have taught that human beings have a soul, or something like it, that makes them unique from other living things. This is not the case in Buddhism. The Buddha taught that all living things are Buddha. Ants, elephants, chimps, rabbits, and dogs all have Buddha nature but in a way that is different from humans.

In some of the earlier sects of Buddhism that developed in India and Southeast Asia, the emphasis was upon the individual monk who lived alone in a forest or mountain seeking to free themselves from the desires that lead us, again and again, into trouble and disappointment. But from the beginning Chan Buddhism, and it's offshoot Zen Buddhism, emphasized community. In Zen Buddhism we say the three treasures of Buddhism are Buddha, Dharma and Sangha. Buddha is a treasure because he showed us the way to free ourselves from fear and anxiety. The Dharma are a treasure because these are teachings that help us find the path. The Sangha is the community of practitioners. The Sangha is a treasure because sitting in community encourages our diligence, our practice, and our understanding. The Sangha is a community in which we can struggle and grow in our practice.

So Chan flourished in China and many monasteries were founded to promote the Dharma.   As it adapted to Chinese culture and incorporated elements of Taoism, Buddhism embraced the Taoist idea of Wu-Wei or non-doing.   The Taoists believed that the universe is evolving as it should be and we should not expect it to be other than it is.   Once we accept this we can harmonize ourselves with the flow of things as they really are, not as we wish them to be or think they should be.   Once we have done this we are no longer fighting the changes of the world.   Instead, we are flowing with them.   It is said the last thing to sink in a storm is a cork and in Buddhism we meditate to attain a similar state.   In Japan when a young monk enters a Zen monastery he is called Unsoi or Cloud-Water. How do clouds and water travel through the world? They flow easily and without effort.   If they encounter an obstacle they bump against it gently and flow around it.   They don't cling or hang on to things if there is an avenue where they can freely flow.   We are like those clouds and that water, we need to only to see that to be free.   These ideas are often an obstacle to those coming to sit Zen for the first time.   In the West we have been taught that everything can be improved. We want to change our partners, change how our job is done, and even change ourselves. Taoism is much more relaxed about all of this. The fundamental insight of Taoism is that the universe is humming along, everything is on schedule, and we should appreciate it as it is. The Taoists see dissatisfaction as simply misunderstanding the wisdom and perfection of the current state of affairs. This Taoist worldview fit perfectly with Buddha's enlightenment statement that all beings are Buddha, full of wisdom and compassion. Buddhism flourished in the soil of China.

The reputation of Chan spread beyond China and monks from other nations traveled to China to study in the mountain monasteries with the great Chan Masters. One of the greatest Japanese Zen Masters, Eihei Dogen Zengi, who lived in the 13th Century, studied Chan Buddhism in China for five years and then brought that wisdom back to Japan and set down the roots of Zen as we know it today. To show the influence that Taoism had on Chinese Ch'an Buddhism, we need only to see what Dogen did as he studied in the Chinese monastery. He was assigned to the kitchen where instead of meditating and seeking enlightenment in silence, he was asked to stoke fires, cook rice, and cut vegetables. By mindfully performing these tasks Dogen deepened his understanding of Buddhism.   He later wrote a work entitled "Instructions to the cook" where he shared what he learned.   In Zen Buddhism paying attention to the simplest tasks is emphasized. Instead of complicated talk about enlightenment, reincarnation or karma we are told we should simply "chop wood, carry water".

Now that Buddhism had incorporated elements of Chinese Taoism it underwent yet another cultural transformation.   When the monks who studied in China returned home to Japan, they wedded their new teaching with the traditional Japanese folk religion of Shintoism. Like most folk religions around the world, Shintoism had shrines to various local gods and friendly spirits that would aid people in times of trouble. Again, like most folk religions around the world, Shintoism had festivals for the equinox, the coming of the New Year, harvest festivals, welcoming of Spring (the famous Cherry Blossom Festival), and a recognition of other seasonal events. Buddhist holidays and traditions were overlaid with these events.

The last cultural influence we need to consider before we get to Hakuin and The Song in Praise of Zazen is Bushido. Bushido is the code of the warriors in Japan that governed their behavior. During the Edo Period, which lasted from 1603-1868. During this time, a warrior class called the Samurai served the various lords of Japan. Zen and Bushido mutually influenced each other. From Zen, the samurai learned to be calm, accept their fate, and meditate while looking inward. From Bushido, Japanese Zen inherited a warrior spirit of quiet determination, discipline in long periods of sitting zazen, and a commitment to the death to strive for enlightenment. We have now journeyed from the founding of Buddhism to the time of Hakuin, the author of the Song in Praise of Zazen.

Hakuin Ekaku

Hakuin Ekaku (1686-1768) was born near the slopes of Mount Fuji. His mother was devoted to Nichiren Buddhism. So at an early age he began his quest of enlightenment and became a monk. For many years he sat in zazen but did not achieve his goal of liberating himself from suffering. He studied many of the sutras, especially the Lotus Sutra. Then at 24 he achieved his first enlightenment. The Japanese word "Kensho" means awakening. In Zen this means freeing yourself from some delusion or compulsion that has hold on you. Some time later Hakuin went to study with the Zen Master Shoju Rojin (1642-1721). Shoju ran a very austere and disciplined monastery and was very tough and demanding of his students. But his harshness and anger were useful in freeing Hakuin from other delusions that he labored under. Shoju helped him see clearly the actual nature of things.

Over time, Hakuin himself became a teacher and a respected figure in Japanese Zen.

In Hakuin's time, Zen had been in decline for some years and had lost its original focus. He is often credited with bringing energy and fire back to Zen. To help his student monks to reach enlightenment he used little puzzles to unlock their minds and free them from the restrictions of logic or habit. These little puzzles are called Koans. All of us are prisoners of our delusions and compulsions. Even the most enlightened of Zen teachers have their delusions. It takes effort to free ourselves from these habits, which we may call our truths but are, in reality, our delusions. Koans are one tool to break these chains. Koan comes from the Chinese term Kung An, which means a public case or something to be put on trial to see the outcome. Koans are used to create great doubt in the student and help the student to overcome this doubt and eventually see things as they really are. I myself once meditated on a single Koan for three years almost continuously until I eventually began to understand what was required of me. We all know little puzzles like this. For example, if you have ever been asked "If a tree falls in the forest and no one hears it, does it make a sound?" or "Are any two snowflakes alike?" you have heard a koan.

Hakuin is credited with inventing the following Koan: "You know the sound of two hands clapping but what is the sound of one hand clapping?" By concentrating on this puzzle, the student eventually gives up looking for a logical solution. When that happens he eventually learns to look directly at things without the help of words or concepts. This is aim of Zen and people who can see directly into the heart of things are said to be enlightened. We will explore the concept of enlightenment as we go through The Song in Praise of Zazen.

There is a story about Hakuin Ekaku that is very well known in Zen circles. It is called "Is That So?" This story is a great demonstration of the Zen attitude that has made it so popular worldwide. Here is the story:

A young Japanese girl whose parents worked in the market lived near the monastery where Hakuin was the teacher. Hakuin was revered and loved in the village. One day the girl's parents discovered she was pregnant. This made her parents angry. Even though they pressed her to answer, the young girl would not tell them who the father was. Finally, she became exhausted and at last named Hakuin as the father of her child. This was a scandal that would bring down the great teacher. In great anger the parents went to the master and told him about the accusation their daughter had made. "Is that so?" was all he would say.

After the child was born, it was brought to Hakuin. By this time he had lost his reputation, which did not trouble him. Instead he devoted himself to taking care of the child. He obtained milk from his neighbors and everything else the child needed. He went on in disgrace and poverty and continued to see that the child lacked nothing.

A year later the girl could stand it no longer. She told her parents the truth - the real father of the child was a young fishmonger from the next town. Hakuin had been innocent all the time but he kept that to himself. He had suffered everything with grace and comportment.

The mother and father of the girl at once went to Hakuin, to apologize at length, and to get the child back. Bowing and crying in shame, they begged his forgiveness. Hakuin willingly yielded the child, saying only: "Is that so?"

This story shows the Zen serenity of Hakuin in the face of ruin and adversity. It shows a composure and equanimity that many Zen practitioners aspire to.

Hakuin thought that a student of Zen could not achieve enlightenment by simply sitting on a cushion. He saw there was a second part to the Zen journey. He said the true student of Zen who deeply seeks liberation must cultivate a deep compassion and commitment to help all sentient beings achieve enlightenment. For Hakuin, the wisdom that is achieved in meditation must be actualized in compassion. There can be no salvation without loving kindness and the realization that all beings are connected by the same thread. It is this marriage of wisdom and compassion that

we will learn about as we study The Song in Praise of Zazen.

PART II- A LINE BY LINE ANALYSIS

Let us begin our analysis with the fantastic claim of the very first line.

1. From the beginning all beings are Buddha.

In some other translations it is said "From the very beginning" and "beings" is sometimes translated as "all sentient beings" or "all living beings".

Before we can decide if this claim is true or false, we must see what it means. The word Buddha is equivocal and has a number of different meanings within our Zen Buddhist tradition. It can refer to a man who long ago gave us a hint about how to escape from

33

suffering. It is can also refer to any enlightened teacher who can show us the way to ease suffering. But here in the first line of this song it refers to the essential nature or energy shared by all beings.

But if all living things are different how can they have the same essential nature? Just as bees and cows and humans and shrimp all share DNA, all living things contain Buddha Nature. This is the nature we are born with. Zen teaches that we are not born cruel or prejudiced, these things must be learned. We are not born fearful or angry, these behaviors are acquired. We are not born mean or stingy, we are educated into these habits. Our Buddha Nature is sometimes called in Zen "our original nature" or "our original face". As an infant looking on the world for the first time, we see it without all of our ideas and theories. As we grew up, our minds became filled with judgements, theories, and opinions. Teachers, religious instruction, history books, relatives, and friends unscrewed our little heads and poured in gallons of judgements and opinions. As our head filled up with all these ideas, it became harder to see things as they are. When this happens we can forget our original nature which is our Buddha Nature. We meditate so we can see things as they truly are, not how we think they should be or should not be. Zen teachers have used terms like "suchness" or "thusness" to refer to things as they are. In our meditation we aim to see clearly or without prejudice.

Line 35, the final line of this song, brings this point home not abstractly but points directly to us. It tells us ME, this very body, is the body of Buddha. It stands to reason that if all beings are Buddha we can assume that whoever is chanting the song is a being and that being is by definition Buddha. We will examine this claim later.

Our Original Nature, our Buddha Nature, which is bright, clear, and luminous, became obscured by the clouds of prejudice and opinion. Eventually our eyeglasses became so thick and dirty we could barely see at all. Our vision is so cloudy that we see the world in terms of good and bad, friends and enemies, us and them. These intellectual constructions prevent us from seeing the world as it is. As a child, I learned that this religious group was good, this race of people was bad, this food was good for you, that food was bad for you, this nation was our friend, and that nation could not be trusted. I was taught to divide the world between us and them, and I learned to watch out for them as soon as I spotted them. And that went for whoever "them" was at the moment. I was not raised in a world of merciful Buddhas but a world in which I was taught to identify men, women, Jews, Blacks, Irish, rich, poor, Indians, and Gypsies. I was taught to see bankers as different from hobos. To really and truly "get" this is to almost be enlightened. I add the caution "almost" because seeing everything as Buddha is not the whole story. We also have to keep in mind that beings appear to be individual to us. So that means that all beings are both Buddha and still appear to be themselves. In another Buddhist chant we say "Leaves that come from the same root". This refers to realizing each thing is uniquely itself while at the same time having Buddha Nature. When both relative and absolute can be seen simultaneously, that is enlightenment. The concept of Enlightenment in Zen is sometimes called Satori or Kensho. When a student achieves this they can be certified by their teacher to be a teacher themselves.

But if you are the average person on the street in 16th Century Japan, it may seem hard to believe that the Shogun, a horse, and a falcon all have the same nature. So if the claim is that ALL BEINGS ARE BUDDHA, how can we illustrate this is true? How can we help people see this? For many serious students of meditation the idea that all is Buddha is hard to grasp. It seems that our differences are more real than the essential nature we share. For some it seems intellectually dishonest to ignore all of the distinctions and head into the oneness of all beings. But the heart of Buddhism is our shared Buddha nature. How can we truly understand this? The answer comes in the next several lines in the form of three analogies. Let us look at analogy number one.

2. Like water and ice, without water no ice.

If you want to see how two things that look different but share the same nature, seeing how water is hidden inside of ice is a good example. At first it might seem like water and ice are different. One is solid and another is liquid. One is frozen and the other is not. One is fixed and the other can flow. Speaking philosophically, we can say they have the same substance or essence but their properties or attributes are different. Considering these differences one might conclude that water and ice do not share the same nature. But that would be incorrect. Just as all beings, which seem different, share Buddha Nature, so ice and water (the analogy) share the nature of water. But water is the hidden nature of ice just as Buddha Nature is the hidden nature of all sentient or living beings. However they do appear to be different at the same time.

The French philosopher Rene Descartes (1596-1650) used a similar analogy to talk about the philosophical concept of substance as opposed to what he called an accident. He noticed how a candle is solid but melted wax is liquid. A candle is cool to touch while melted wax is hot. A candle has shape but melted wax does not. With so many differences he wondered how they could share the same name. Hakuin's analogy is meant to show us how difference and identity are not contradictions but complimentary.

This first analogy supports the important claim in line 1. that ALL BEINGS ARE BUDDHA. But there is an additional aspect to this first analogy that relates directly to our Zen training. Zen training has historically been very hard because it has been an effort to liberate our Buddha Nature from the shackles and fog of our delusions, illusions, opinions, and prejudices. The Sensei or Zen teacher might use questions to break down the students defenses and help them breakthrough to enlightenment. Heat is what is needed to liberate or free water from ice. In the same way the teacher or Sensei wants to free the student from their frozen opinions and prejudices.

The concept of water has an echo in the Taoist roots of Chinese Chan Buddhism. The bible of Taoism, the Tao Te Ching, was written by Lao Tzu. For Lao Tzu, water is the metaphor for the path we all walk on. Water has a genius for flowing around obstacles and eventually reaches its goal. But by going around and over these obstacles it does not surrender to them. In time water wears down the hardest rock. The Grand Canyon is a testament to the power of gentle water and wind. Water never has to force its way. It finds the easiest and most gentle solution to every encounter. This is how the Unsoi or cloud-water monk floats through life, never getting hung up or stopped. Lao Tzu praises the genius of water. Let me paraphrase his words from the Tao Te Ching:

The Tao is like water. It benefits all and never uses force, It dwells in the lowest places that others do not value. Be like water and you will walk the path of the Tao. When living, be gentle to the earth. Like water seek what is deepest. When you hit a boulder, go around it.

Thus this analogy of water and ice in line two supports the initial claim of Line 1. So where are we to look for Buddhas? Not in heaven or the sky but right around us. This sets up Line 3 which follows from Line 2.

3. Outside us no Buddhas.

Just as water is the secret hidden inside of ice, so Buddha is the secret inside each and every one of us. Buddha Nature is not something to be achieved in another lifetime or another dimension. It is not something we will be in the future. It is not something to be attained. You and I are Buddhas right here and right now. In many religions there is talk of heaven or hell sometime in the future. Other religions are preparing us for some future perfection. But in Zen all we have to do is open our eyes and wake up. Line 3 connects the analogy of water and ice to Buddhas and ourselves. The Buddha here does not refer to a far away god living in peace and happiness. It is us, here and now, with toothaches, financial worries, and relationship issues, trying to find our way. In my anger, anxiety, depression, and confusion I am Buddha. When I am happy I am Buddha, and when I am sad I am Buddha. I was Buddha at seventeen when I was strong and agile, and I will be Buddha at ninety taking my blood pressure medication. We don't need to look elsewhere for the Buddha, because we are Buddha. In many of our Buddhist writings there is the phrase "right here and right now". There is no need to wait for paradise. In Buddhism the word for suffering is "Samsara" and the word for release from suffering is "Nirvana". It can be said that in Zen, Samsara and Nirvana are the same. We don't seek to escape from the world but to fully inhabit it. Rather than fighting the present moment and wishing we were elsewhere, we should embrace it. But to fully embrace our nature is to embrace it in all of its flaws, suffering, and blisters. Only by saying a firm "Yes" to all of life do we have the chance to stay in the present and, by doing that ,inhabit our Buddha Nature. If there is no Buddha outside of us, then our words and deeds are the manifestation of Buddha. Every step we take is a step in the footprints of the Buddha. We should bring our eyes down from the heavens, stop worrying about life after death, and be right here right now.

4. How near the truth, yet how far we seek.

If there are no Buddhas outside of us, then must begin our search by looking close at hand. We must start from where we are, not where we want to go. So often we are entangled in things that are far from us. We worry about the lives of movie stars or the decisions of political figures that we will never meet. We worry about things that never happen. We regret past events we can no longer relive or change. People seek happiness not within themselves but in the possession and enjoyment of external things. We desire new cars, new furniture, changes of fashion, and we struggle to keep up with these desires. Buddhism tells us that those things will not make us happy. Things will not fill up our lives. Anything that will give us pleasure by its possession can cause pain by its loss. Don't think of the cycle of rebirth in terms of our lifetimes but the rebirth of suffering caused by the gaining and loss of external things. To achieve enlightenment we need to redirect our gaze. Instead of looking far away and outside, we should turn our eyes to what is right in front of us and begin our journey here.

The first line of The Song in Praise of Zazen tells us that all beings are Buddha. If that is the case we don't need to seek anywhere for what is right here. To find enlightenment we need only to still our desires for the past and future. Remember, the word Buddha means "to awaken". This means we need to stay focused on ourselves in the present moment. The best way to do that is by sitting Zazen. In the Soto Zen tradition we say that when we sit Zazen we literally are Buddha.

5. Like one in water crying I thirst.

We find here the third mention of "water" in Hakuin's song. In our first two uses of the word, water was identified with our Buddha Nature. This line echoes the first two uses but now we see that Buddha nature is all around us. It is not to be sought outside of us. Fish only understand water when they leave it. While they are swimming in it, it is simply what is in front of them. Some people thirst for enlightenment. Others thirst to be released from the endless cycle of wanting, having, and losing. We might thirst to live a happy, calm life. We often search for these things outside of us. We already possess everything we need but instead we are looking elsewhere for what is right in front of us. But how is it we do not know we are in water when we thirst? This line and the next line tells us it is a kind of forgetfulness that keeps us from knowing our own nature. There is a tension in Zen teachings about striving and just being. If we are already Buddha there is no need to strive. At the same time the Japanese warrior ethic of Bushido urges us to make strong effort to break through the delusions and compulsions that hold us back from seeing clearly.

If we can take the time to sit and just breathe the clouds should disperse and over time we can see. Sadly, there is no schedule or path to enlightenment. There is a tradition in Zen that talks of sudden enlightenment which means that no one can predict when our minds will open to the beauty of the here and now.

6. Like a son of rich birth, wandering poor on this earth.

There are several stories from the history of Buddhism connected with this line. The first comes from the Lotus Sutra. It tells of a wealthy man from India who lived long ago. He had a young son who one day disappeared. The man mourned for a long time and many years passed. Then one day a beggar in rags appeared at the gate of the rich man's palace. The man recognized the beggar as his long lost son. When the rich man approached him, the beggar fled in fear thinking he had done something wrong. So the rich man sent a servant after the beggar and convinced him to come work for him in the fields. Over time, the beggar came to work in the house. Eventually he managed the rich man's estate and finances. When the rich man was very old, he called together his staff and announced that the beggar was in reality the son he had lost and would inherit the estate.

There is a similar story told in the Zen tradition. A rich man loses his memory and does not realize he is wealthy. So he descends into poverty and becomes a beggar. A little while later he reaches into an inside pocket in his dirty robe and finds a very expensive gem that has been there all of the time. Like the beggar in our first story, he was rich all of the time but did not know it. But all the time he had in his possession the means of his release from poverty and want. He didn't need to look outside of himself. He didn't need to get anything from anyone that he did not already have. We are all born with Buddha Nature. We are all born with all the wisdom and compassion we need to be released from suffering. We don't need to go to Tibet, Kyoto, or India to find ourselves. We only need to reach into our own pockets and we will see it has been there all the time.

7. We endlessly circle the six worlds.

Zen Buddhism is attractive to many Americans and Europeans because it does not ask us to accept things on faith. We can find out for ourselves by looking inward. Prior to all of the teaching, all of the sutras, and all the oral tradition, there is the admonition by the Buddha that we should rely on our own experience. Faith plays so little a role that sometimes people ask if Zen Buddhism is a religion. I answer this question by saying I don't know if it is a religion or not, but it is first and foremost a technique of liberation. Line 7 takes us to that place where religion, folklore, and faith intersect with experience, doubt, and skepticism.

In some Buddhist traditions and some countries the six worlds (sometimes called the six realms) are thought of as actual places where people are reincarnated based on their actions in past lives. Karma is the name given to the residual from every action we take. Like physics, in the moral world every action creates a reaction. Karma is not limited to Eastern philosophy but an idea generally found in every culture and every age. The Bible tell us that you reap what you sow. Charles Dickens had a ghost appear to the miser Ebenezer Scrooge that was bound with chains and dragging heavy account books. This is because in life that ghost was Scrooge's business partner Jacob Marley who put the profits of his business above morality and compassion. In many cultures around the world there are stories of ghosts of ancestors who assist us and those who could do us harm. That is why there are prohibitions about handling the dead in many cultures because there is the idea that, to quote Shakespeare in his play Julius Caesar, the evil men do is often remembered after their deaths. In many cultures there is a day or time of year when those spirits can return to the world. Often these festivals happen around harvest time as a metaphor for the dying of the crops. In Japan, the festival of Obon is celebrated in August with lanterns and bonfires to guide the spirits back home. Mexico's Day of the Dead (el Día de los Muertos) uses masks and music to call the spirits. In America we celebrate Halloween because that is the night of year in the Christian Calendar between All Souls Day and All Saints Day when the veil between the worlds of the living and dead is the thinnest.

The Zen tradition, as it has evolved from India, to China, to Japan, and now to the West, has a strong agnostic element. As practitioners of American Zen we look at the six worlds not as actual places but as metaphors for ways to live our lives and the consequences each choice makes. The six worlds are sometimes portrayed as a wheel where we migrate from one world to the other. The journey around the wheel is called Samsara which is the succession of birth and death and keeps us going in circles. This going in circles eventually causes us to suffer and this suffering is called Dukkha. The birth and death that is spoken of here is the birth and death of our desires. A desire is born, grows, and eventually dies before another desire is born to take its place. The trick is how to liberate ourselves from this merry-go-round.

The six worlds are the World of Hell, the World of Hungry Ghosts, the World of Animals, the World of the Demi Gods, the World of the gods, and the World of Humans. The World of Humans, oddly enough, is the highest, and later on we will see why. Let us look at these worlds as metaphors for states of being we might find ourselves or others in.

The World of Hell (Naraka-gati) is marked by anger and frustration. Anger, along with greed and ignorance, make up the three poisons. Anger arises from thinking things should be other than they are. Anger is often connected to fear. Anger is the opposite of acceptance. Anger poisons our body and releases chemicals that are harmful for the person who is angry. Because the angry person is always fighting against what is real, their anger can become the most important thing in their lives. Domestic abuse and substance abuse are often linked to anger. To live in anger is to be in a state of agitation. By sitting Zazen we attempt to transform anger into compassion.

How do we transform anger into compassion? When we mediate, be it sitting or being mindful at any time, we want to pay attention to our habits and reactions. We want to notice when anger arises, when greed arises, when we become anxious, or when we become disturbed. Any of these states can hijack our mind and throw us right into the Hell of Anger and Fear. When we sit in silence we can build up Samadhi, which is the power we get from meditation, just like we get muscles from going to the gym. That Samadhi can help up catch anger and fear as they begin to emerge and before they have a grip on our mind. We can then work on composting that anger into love and compassion.

The World of Hungry Ghosts (Preta-gati) is about those who are constantly hungry for new things. Hungry ghosts have small mouths but great big stomachs so they must constantly feed but never are satisfied. There is no such thing as "enough" for them. Many of us live as Hungry Ghosts. These people seek for happiness in new cars, new fashions and new relationships. The concept of Hungry Ghosts can help us understand alcoholics, drug addicts, and those among us with eating disorders. The hunger prevents these beings from sitting still long enough to realize that their hunger cannot be quenched and so they wander on in search of what they will not find, peace.

The concept of hungry ghosts is also found in Taoism where it is said that these were the ghosts of those that lived a life of excess or committed some crime or sin. So to be reborn as a hungry ghost is a punishment but it is not for all eternity. In Buddhism there is always the chance to move to another spot on the Wheel of Samsara if we learn the lesson and change our ways. However some hungry ghosts are stuck for a long time, not having the self insight to change their ways.

How many of us live our lives chasing things that will not make us happy? We will find out later in the Song in Praise of Zazen that this land where we stand is the pure Lotus Land. If we are already Buddha, chasing external things will not satisfy us. Many of us have a hole inside of us we are trying to fill. Those people, whose stomachs are too big and mouths are too small, can never fill the whole no matter how hard they try.

The next stage is the World of Animals (Tiryagoni-gati). Animals live by impulse and instinct. They are slaves to whatever comes into their view. Toss a stick and some dogs have no choice but to chase it. If you threw that stick in a raging river the dog would go in to retrieve it before he realized what he had done. Shine a light on the wall and some cats will try to grab it for hours. They can't help themselves. When a cat sees a mouse or a bird they instinctively snap into hunting mode. Because they are ignorant, they are bound by their feelings which they cannot escape. One day I was sitting on a second story balcony with my cat. He saw a lizard in a tree. Without thought for his own safety, he lept through the bars of the railing and hung from a branch high in the air. He was terrified before I rescued him. He did not think of the consequences because he could not help himself. How many people we know are slaves to some emotion or idea that rules their life? This is the World of Animals

Next is the World of the Demi-Gods (Asura-gati). Even though they have supernatural powers they are driven by greed and envy of the devas or gods. Envy and greed are born out of feelings of inferiority. This is desire to get to the front of the line and in the process put others down. This is a world where we measure ourselves against others and always come up short. In Buddhism it is said "Do not seek after truth, only seek not to cherish opinions". But in the World of Demi-Gods, there is always the constant jockeying for first place. Battles between siblings, business partners, political foes, lovers are all driven by wrongly comparing ourselves to others. This is the world of rivalry that many of us have lived in. Who is the daughter who is most loved? Which Executive Vice President is in line to be the next CEO? Whose lawn looks more manicured? Who has the nicest car or clothes? Who has the most plastic surgery at the high school reunion? Many of us are jockeying to move up and get ahead of others. The contest of who is number one has no end and no good ending. It is the cause of anger, resentment, and argument. This the world of the Demigods.

The World of the Gods (Deva-gati). The Gods have it all. There is no need to work. There is no illness. There is wealth. There is pleasure. It would seem this is perfection. In many other cultures this is a description of Heaven or Paradise. But for a Buddhist this is not the best realm to be reborn into. This is a realm of laziness and attachments. Surrounded by pleasure, wealth, and beauty you would think you would never want to leave. But isn't that exactly what Buddha did when he left his palace and life of comfort behind? Money and pleasure can shield one from the suffering of others. It can make one calloused and self-centered. The rich are sometimes oblivious to the poor. So the World of Gods is not the best spot of the wheel. There is one higher and that is the World of Humans.

The World of Humans (Manusya-gati) is the best realm to be born in. Why would this be better than the World of the Gods surrounded by pleasure without any pain? Because in the World of Humans we have the Dharma, the Sangha, and the Buddha. We can do Zazen. We can chant the sutras. We can learn and change. We have the possibility to be released from the wheel of birth and death. It is sometimes said in the Zen literature that hearing the Dharma just once, or sitting Zazen just one time, can bring mountains of merit and endless benefits. How lucky we are to have the obstacles that can teach us. How fortunate we are that we have the self reflective powers to change and improve our lives. In this "reincarnation" or life we have access to the tools that can take us off the Wheel of Samsara, the tools to free us from birth and death and get off the merry-go-round. This is why the human world is the most desirous for Buddhists, because in this world we have the power to improve our lives.

We can then summarize the six worlds in this way:

World of Humans--The three poisons of Greed, Anger and Ignorance, but we can hear the Dharma and free ourselves from the wheel of suffering.

World of the Gods--Ignoring suffering. The poison of Ignorance.

World of the Demi-Gods--Jealousy. The poison of Greed.

World of Animals--Lack of knowledge. The poison of Ignorance.

World of Hungry Ghosts--Compulsion and Addiction. The poison of Greed.

World of Hell--Anger. The poison of Anger.

The six worlds we circle can be read as our lives steered by greed, anger, fear, compulsions, and ignorance. Once we are in the grip of one of these states our reason is not clear and we do not see the truth. Anger makes us say and do things we regret later. Ignorance keeps us locked in our old patterns even if we can't help it. Compulsions and addictions ruin lives because those in the grip of addiction sometimes feel like they cannot help themselves. Greed puts us in a constant state of comparison, competition, and battling which can be emotionally painful. Ignorance keeps us spinning on the wheel over and over again. But there is way to free ourselves and later, in Line 11, we will learn that "The gateway to freedom is Zazen Samadhi".

8. The cause of our sorrow is ego delusion.

How is it that beings are stuck on the Wheel of Samsara? Why don't they figure this out and change their behaviors? Why are some people self destructive? Why do people say and do things they later regret? Why do people ingest substances that harm their bodies? Why do we hurt the ones we love? The answer to all of these questions is the same, and that answer is ignorance. Zen teaches that if we became conscious of things we were doing that hurt ourselves and others we would stop doing them. Alcoholics Anonymous, Gamblers Anonymous, Drug Addicts Anonymous, Sex Addicts Anonymous and all the rest talk about their condition as a disease. In Zen Buddhism there is only one disease, and one disease alone. That disease is ego delusion. Ego delusion is a very specific kind of ignorance. Let us dissect this term. Ego, which comes from the Greek word for "I", means I am separate from everyone and everything else. Ego means I am disconnected from everything else. Because I am disconnected this means that things I like or dislike are believed to be outside of me and different from me. I am a solid separate being that is different from, and separated from, all other beings. I am as unique as the mythical snowflake that has no twin.

The second term is delusion. A delusion is something we think to be the case but is not true. So believing we are separate from everything is a mistake that causes us "sorrow" as the line says. If all is Buddha and we are Buddha there is nothing to resist, fight against, or chase after. We all have all we need right within us at any given moment. Not knowing this we waste our time chasing after things outside of ourselves that will not make us happy. This line is an expansion of the thought in Lines 3 thru 6.

How near the truth, yet how far we seek

Like one in water crying I thirst (5)

Like a son of rich birth, wandering poor on this earth.

Because we do not understand the truth is near and seek it elsewhere it leads to sorrow. So looking outward is a key mistake brought on by our delusion that we, as an ego, are separate from the world. Next we ask why is this delusion bad for us? Line 9 answers this question.

9. From dark path to dark path we've wandered in darkness.

Line 7 mentions the six worlds. Beings remain in the one of the six worlds because of ego delusion which is a specific kind of ignorance. Some of the six worlds are better than others but beings are held to all of them by some version of ego delusion. Anger, greed, fear, compulsion, and ignorance are the dark paths we have wandered in darkness. This is a wheel of birth and death, sometimes called the wheel of Karma or the wheel of reincarnation. We endlessly circle the six worlds but are stumbling from path to path in the darkness of ignorance. Now that we realize that we are going around in circles that leads us to a question. In many Zen stories the moon, a candle, or a lantern are elements. This is because when we open our eyes, the dark paths will disappear. In Line 31 of this song we hear "How bright and transparent the moonlight of wisdom". It is the moon that gives its light to make the dark paths disappear.

10. How can we be free from birth and death?

Line 10 breaks away from the first 9 lines and asks us how we can realize the truth of Line 1 that "From the beginning, all beings are Buddha". As long as we think we are separate from the world, we circle the six worlds containing anger, ignorance, and greed. Anger, ignorance, and greed are sometimes called the Three Unwholesome Roots or the Three Poisons in Buddhism. These Three Poisons have a hold on us because of our ego delusion. They are the root of craving for things outside of ourselves that keep us from looking inward. As long as our gaze is directed outward and we whirl in motion, driven by our desires, we remain in Samsara where our fears and hopes are born, die, and are reborn. The Three Poisons create the Karma that is the glue that keeps us spinning on the Wheel of Samsara.

The Three Poisons can be countered by practicing The Three Wholesome Qualities: Wisdom (Prajna), Generocity (Dana), and Loving Kindness (Metta). We will examine these in detail later in the work.

11. The gateway to freedom is Zazen Samadhi

The best way to free ourselves from the Wheel of Samsara is to sit in meditation. But we must sit with patience. Line 11 does not say Zazen or sitting meditation will give you freedom. It says the GATEWAY to freedom is Zazen SAMADHI. It is the gateway because there is a second element to our journey towards freedom. That second element is living a good life by observing the precepts. The precepts are the ethical rules that students of the Dharma follow to help them live a life in accordance with the Buddha's way. But it all starts from just sitting.

Sitting Zazen is the heart of Zen practice. The aim of Zen Buddhism is liberation from the glue that holds us to the worlds of anger, ignorance, and greed. This liberation is not some intellectual trick. It is done by sitting steadily in silence. Just as your muscles improve with exercise, as we sit over time we build up our ability to concentrate. Our aim is to be in a state of Samadhi which is the Sanskrit word for "total self absorption". As we sit over time, our restless energy settles down. We build up the ability to meditate over a longer period of time. In Samadhi we are slowly freed from anxiety and fear. When we are in a state of samadhi we are free from time and space because we are only in the here and now. Samadhi is a precondition for release from the six worlds but it alone is not enough. We must also align our life with the Dharma. But not everyone that sits builds up Samadhi. This is not an automatic given. To do this we must examine and let go of the three poisons of greed, anger, and ignorance. We must hold fast and sit "like a mountain". This is not easy and there are no shortcuts. It is a long and sometimes difficult commitment. But the reward is something truly special.

12. Beyond exaltation, beyond all our praises, the pure Mahayana.

Mahayana literally means The Great Vehicle. Rather than focusing on the liberation or enlightenment of a single person, it seeks the liberation of all beings. For this reason compassion is as important as wisdom for this tradition. Mahayana is the general name for the teachings for many schools of Buddhism including Chinese Ch'an, Japanese Zen, Japanese Pure Land, Korean Seon, Tendai, Shingon Buddhism, and Tibetan Buddhism.

Mahayana is another name for the Bodhisattvayana (Bodhisattva Vehicle). A Bodhisattva is a person who is able to reach enlightenment but delays doing so out of loving kindness so that he can return to the world to save suffering beings. Instead of living in the bliss of Nirvana (which we will discuss in Line 33) the Bodhisattva turns his back on his or her own happiness and instead teaches the dharma to all beings. The goal is help all beings realize their enlightenment.

In many Zendos, the community or Sangha chants the Bodhisattva's vow:

Creations are numberless, I vow to free them

Delusions are inexhaustible, I vow to transform them

Reality is boundless, I vow to perceive it,

The enlightened way is unsurpassable, I vow to embody it.

What a bold promise, to free all creations! What a wild idea that we can save every single being. But this may not be so difficult if we remember what we learned in Line 1 of the Song in Praise of Zazen. From the beginning, all beings are Buddha. This means that there is no need to teach a long and complex doctrine. Beings only need a gentle reminder to reignite their Buddha nature. Like straw that is dry and smoldering we only need a spark to bring back the fire.

We all have within us all that we need to escape from suffering and live in bliss. It also tells us that all beings are already Buddha.

Thus, the Bodhisattva becomes a vehicle by which other sentient beings ride to enlightenment. Think of a firefighter who would give up their own life to save a person they never met. Think of a doctor who enters a country with a raging epidemic. That is the Bodhisattva's way.

This means that the Bodhisattva can use any device if it will awake the sleeping dreamer. To help other beings see their true nature, the Bodhisattva uses Upaya or expedient means. The words Upaya-Kaushalya can be translated into English as Expedient Means. This means that the teacher recognizes that each student in different so they adopt their teaching lesson to the student and situation. Using Upaya-Kaushalya it may be necessary to sometimes even go against the teachings of the Buddha. There is a story in the Second Chapter of The Lotus Sutra about a man who uses a lie to get his children out of a burning house.   Saving their lives was more important than telling the truth.   Expedient Means is used to explain all of the strange stories of Zen Masters striking their students, shouting instead of speaking and, in some stories, killing cats or cutting off fingers. Of course these stories are metaphorical and not to be taken literally. These stories are meant to show how the teacher finds out where the student is and what will appeal to them at that moment

Turning one's back on Nirvana and returning to the realm of suffering is a great personal sacrifice. But the Bodhisattva realizes that all beings are one and his salvation is their salvation, so compassion is the key element in Mahayana. For the Mahayana, wisdom (Prajna) is actualized in acts of compassion (Karuna). Because there is no self, there is a motivation to save all beings. By saving other beings I am saving myself. In the Diamond Sutra we are told that beings are not innumerable and distinct. They are in fact all the same essence, Buddha. That is just the illusion in the same way that the nature of water is hidden in ice.

If all beings are Buddha then judging some good and some bad makes no sense. Our compassion arises from not discriminating and using the words "good" or "bad". Our compassion arises from our knowing that we are brother and sister, father and mother, son and daughter to everything that is. Not just all living things but all beings. We should treat our tools with respect. We should honor the earth that feeds us. We should thank the stones from which our house is built. It has been said that even a stone can be a teacher. This is true for all things for they all carry with them the light of the Buddha.

A great Zen Master once said "Do not seek truth, only cease from discriminating". Once you do that you are in harmony with all that is, and at ease with all that is. Once you come into harmony with all beings and cease to cherish some and dislike others you will see the Buddha nature in all things. You then realize that the world of change (Samsara) and the world of bliss (Nirvana) are one in the same. We will see in one of the last lines that "This land where you stand is the pure Lotus Land". But this is not yet enlightenment. Realizing all beings are Buddha is only half the journey. For there are two truths in Buddhism, the absolute and the relative.

Even though all beings are Buddha, salt and sugar taste different. An elephant is larger that a mouse. Fire is hot and water is wet.

So to say simply all is one is only to see one side of the coin. Line 2 of the Song of Praise of Zazen tells us; Like water and ice, without water no ice. While water and ice share the same nature they are different. Ice and water are different and we must respect that. That is the relative truth of their existence. The absolute truth is that we are all Buddha. The relative truth is that if you put your hand on a hot stove it will burn you. That is true even though you both share Buddha Nature.

Back to bodhisattvas. Six pāramitās are traditionally required for bodhisattvas:

1. *dāna-pāramitā*: the perfection of giving

2. *śīla-pāramitā*: the perfection of self control

3. *kṣānti-pāramitā*: the perfection of patience

4. *vīrya-pāramitā*: the perfection of energy

5. *dhyāna-pāramitā*: the perfection of meditation

6. *prajñā-pāramitā*: the perfection of great wisdom

By practicing these virtues we refine our understanding and clear our minds. These are steps on the stairway of liberation.

13. Observing the Precepts, Repentance and Giving,

In some Zen traditions there are sixteen Bodhisattva Precepts that are part of the teaching. When a student accepts these precepts and promises to live in accordance with them we call this ceremony Jukai. Ju is Japanese for taking or accepting and Kai is the Japanese word for precepts. Let us look at the precepts one at time to see what exactly we are taking refuge in. First are the Three Treasures or Refuges.

1. I take refuge in the Buddha
2. I take refuge in the Dharma
3. I take refuge in the Sangha

The Buddha represents Wisdom, the Dharma represents Compassion and the Sangha represents Harmony. The Buddha is the unborn perfection that abides in the emptiness inside of all of us.

It is the shimmering brightness that is revealed once we stop making judgments and imposing our ideas on what we experience. The Buddha is a flower in springtime, a bird singing after a rainstorm and the reflection of the moon in still water. It is the glowing here and now, the eternal THIS. We sit Zazen to be awake enough to see this unfolding brilliance. Enlightenment is when we go beyond words, judgements, and prejudices and we are fully present and fully awake.

To take refuge in the Dharma is to be attentive to the teachings of Buddhism. Because Zen has at its heart sitting meditation we are not asked to accept anything on faith. We must experience things for ourselves. However, the teachings can act a guide as we deepen our practice and look inwards. As Zen Buddhists we are part of a tradition that is thousands of years old. In that time, a great deal of wisdom and profound teaching has been accumulating. We should use every tool we can to reach enlightenment. Remember the Mahayana promises we can attain enlightenment in one lifetime if we apply ourselves. The Dharma are books of shortcut notes to help us achieve this end.

To take refuge in the Sangha means that we can commune with others of like mind. The Sangha is the community where we meditate. But like all communities there can be political differences, personal conflicts, and heated differences of opinion. At the same time it a place where we want to feel safe and supported. Sangha is important because a community can help us maintain discipline, continue our growth, and refine our practice. The Sangha has to be a place where harmony rules.

Next come the Three Pure Precepts.

Pure Precepts

1. I vow to refrain from all evil.

2. I vow to make every effort to do good.

3. I vow to act to save all beings.

The Three Pure Precepts sum up the peaceful and positive way of life that the Buddha laid out for us. The first vow is that we refrain from harming other beings as much as possible. The Buddhists use the terms "living beings" or "sentient beings" to remind us that animals, plants and inanimate objects should be treated with the same love and compassion that we treat human beings. In many religious traditions, humans have a special place above the animal and vegetable realms. This is not the case in Buddhism. In Line 1 we are told that all beings are Buddha. So we must refrain from harming any being. This first Pure Precept is a beginning but not enough.

The Second Pure Precept is not just to refrain from doing evil but to positively do good. This means carrying your practice out of the Zendo into the world. Sitting Zen should settle our anxieties and our fears. As this happens our Samadhi or sitting power grows as our restlessness goes away. The next step is to carry our good energy out of the Zendo and into the world. We should carry our joy out into the world. Just as the Bodhisattva brought Buddhism from India to China, it is up to us to bring Buddhism to the world. As Zen practitioners in the Mahayana tradition.

The Third Pure Precept reminds us once again of our Mahayana tradition which is all about sharing our insights and calm. It reminds us to bring our Zen out of the Zendo and into the world as we work to enlighten all beings.

Next we look at the 10 grave precepts.

Grave Precepts

1. I recognize that I am not separate from all that is. This is the practice of Non-killing. I will not lead a harmful life, nor encourage others to do so. I will live in harmony with all life and the environment that sustains it.

2. I will be satisfied with what I have. This is the practice of Non-stealing. I will freely give, ask for, and accept what is needed.

3. I will encounter all creations with respect and dignity. This is the practice of Chaste Conduct. I will give and accept love and friendship without clinging.

4. I will speak the truth and deceive no one. This is the practice of Non-lying. I will speak from the heart. I will see and act in accordance with what is.

5. I will cultivate a mind that sees clearly. This is the practice of Not Being Deluded. I will not encourage others to be deluded. I will embrace all experience directly.

6. I will unconditionally accept what each moment has to offer. This is the practice of Not Talking About Others Errors and Faults. I will acknowledge responsibility for everything in my life.

7. I will speak what I perceive to be the truth without guilt or blame. This is the practice of Not Elevating Myself and Blaming Others. I will give my best effort and accept the results.

8. I will use all of the ingredients of my life. This is the practice of Not Being Stingy. I will not foster a mind of poverty in myself or others.

9. I will transform suffering into wisdom. This is the practice of Not Being Angry. I will not harbor resentment, rage, or revenge. I will roll all negative experience into my practice.

10. I will honor my life as an instrument of peacemaking. This is the practice of Not Thinking Ill of the Three Treasures. I will recognize myself and others as manifestations of Oneness, Diversity and Harmony.

These are the 10 grave precepts as recited by some sanghas of the White Plum Lineage. The language is distinctly modern and moderate. Below is an older version of the 10 grave precepts which gives a little less "wiggle room" for unethical behavior by Zen Buddhist standards.

1. I vow not to kill.

2. I vow not to take what is not given.

3. I vow not to misuse sexuality.

4. I vow to refrain from false speech.

5. I vow to refrain from intoxicants.

6. I vow not to slander.

7. I vow not to praise self at the expense of others.

8. I vow not to be avaricious.

9. I vow not to harbor ill will

10. I vow not to disparage the Three Treasures.

14. the countless good deeds and the way of right living, all come from zazen.

We must recall that the title of this work is the Song In Praise of Zazen. Sitting Meditation, Zazen, is the very heart of our practice. Everything else flows from this. While we follow the precepts, they are meant as an adjunct to our sitting Zazen. The precepts are not lived in isolation from our sitting meditation. Our ethics arise from our meditation. But this flow is natural. Once we settle our energy by sitting we build up Samadhi which is a kind of spiritual power and this acts as a shield against the ups and downs of life. In this calm state we forget or lose our attachment to a solid and abiding self. Once this flow of experience is felt we see a connection between us and our cushion, between us and the room we sit in and a connection between us and others. In time we see the connection between all beings. What I do to another comes back to myself. Anger hurts me more than it does the person I am angry at. As I see this my solid isolated self is seen in relationship to others. Wisdom (prajna) gives birth to compassion and compassion (Karuna) gives rise to wisdom. As we sit with correct posture and deepen our breathing our aim is become more compassionate. The way of right living can be summarized in the Eightfold Noble Path:

THE NOBLE EIGHTFOLD PATH
1. Right view (Samma ditthi)
2. Right thought (Samma sankappa)
3. Right speech (Samma vaca)
4. Right action (Samma kammanta)
5. Right livelihood (Samma ajiva)
6. Right effort (Samma vayama)

7. Right mindfulness (Samma sati)
8. Right concentration (Samma samadhi)

For thousands of years, Buddhists have lived their lives guided by these eight rules. We can apply them to our lives the instant we see them. When I see Right Speech I am reminded of all of the times I have gossiped, slandered others, and used unkind and vulgar words. Immediately, I can see where I have fallen short and where I need to put my attention to improve. The other seven elements of the The Noble Eightfold Path are equally clear and simple to apply. We sit so that we become vessels to carry these principles into our life.

15. Thus one true samadhi extinguishes evils. It purifies karma, dissolving obstructions.

We have already noted that Samadhi is the power that comes from sitting meditation. After some time of sitting our energy settles and our minds should not race as much. As we meditate we begin to be free of the three poisons of Anger, Greed, and Ignorance. As we grow in our Samadhi we should begin to let go of our negative emotions and become more calm and relaxed. As this happens our old Karma gets "purified". As we recognize the damage we have done to others and, more importantly, to ourselves it becomes clear that we are often our own worst enemy. It is not the universe that has thwarted our plans it is often our own Karma.

16. Then where are the dark paths to lead us astray?

Once the three poisons are identified we can become conscious of the fact that it is wrong to follow them. In the history of Western Philosophy there have been two theories about evil or how we do wrong. Plato theorized that all wrong or evil is done out of ignorance. He argued this because he said that acting this way ultimately hurts others and ends up hurting ourselves, Plato reasoned no one in their right mind would willingly and knowingly harm themselves. So, like Buddha, he reasoned that any wrongdoing happens out of ignorance. Once we realize that we are harming ourselves we would stop such actions. Plain and Simple! Aristotle, on the other hand, believed that we can know something is wrong and still do it because of what he called weakness of the will. He notes that while the mind has opinions, the body itself may have desires that are not entirely rational. An example would be an addict of some sort who might know their habit is ruining their life but feels powerless to stop the progress of the disease. Buddhism is firmly in the camp that knowledge can change behavior.

17. The Pure Lotus Land is not far away.

The lotus flower represents enlightenment in Buddhism. The lotus plant grows in muddy water, and it is this environment that gives forth the flower's first and most literal meaning: rising and blooming above the murk to achieve enlightenment. As the roots go down into the mud, the flower reaches up to the sun. Without the dirt of the mud we would not see the beauty of the lotus. Without our life of suffering and frustration we would not forge on towards enlightenment.

The second meaning, which is related to the first, is purification. The lotus resembles the purifying of the spirit which is born into murkiness. The third meaning of the lotus refers to faithfulness. Those who are working to rise above the muddy waters will need to be faithful followers.

The color bears importance in the meaning of the lotus flower in Buddhism. A white lotus flower refers to purity of the mind and the spirit. If a lotus flower is red, it refers to compassion and love. The blue lotus flower refers to common sense; it uses wisdom and logic to create enlightenment. The pink lotus flower represents the history of Buddha and the historical legends of the Buddha. A purple lotus flower speaks of spiritual awakening and mysticism. Finally, the gold lotus flower represents all achievement of all enlightenment, especially in the Buddha.

The Lotus Land is a mythical place of perfection. It is heaven on earth. In Tibetan Buddhism, part of our Mahayana lineage, there is the story of Shangri La, a mysterious land hidden in the mountains of Tibet. There all is peace and calm. People never grow old and there is no conflict.

What Line 17 suggests is that the Lotus Land is not in the Himalayan Mountains. It is close at hand. Like the early lines about the man in water crying I thirst and child of rich birth, we find that what we seek is right under our feet. There is no place else to go and there is no time we need to get there. All that we need is right in front of us right now at this very second. Line 34 will make this clear.

18. Hearing this truth, heart humble and grateful.

What is the truth that we hear? All beings are Buddha. Outside us no Buddha. All is revealed in the here and now. Nothing in the present moment is lacking. Hearing this truth we should be grateful because other beings such as animals do not have the opportunity to hear the dharma and be freed from the wheel of suffering and rebirth. We should be humble in order to be open and be able to listen with our heart to the teaching of the dharma.

19. To praise and embrace it, to practice its wisdom,

Line 19 urges the practitioner to embrace Zazen, to have faith in the process. While Zen does not ask for faith in the teachings or doctrines it does ask for faith in the practice of meditation. The concept of faith that was a central focus in Chinese Chan Buddhism was replaced by the concept of effort when Zen arrived in Japan and encompassed the Japanese ideas of Bushido, the warrior code of the Samurai class. The gentle encouragement of some of the early and more poetic mountain Chan teachers was replaced with a work ethic that emphasized overcoming pain, fighting through long periods of sitting, and battling our demons in the same way a Samurai Warrior would battle his opponents.

20. brings unending blessings. bring mountains of merit.

What is the reward for sitting through all of the doubt and pain? In Line 20 we are told it brings unending blessings and "mountains" of merit. Before we congratulate ourselves on this pot of gold at the end of the Zen rainbow, let us recall that merit is a term in Buddhism that is more complicated that in most religions. Let us illustrate this by story.

The Bodhidharma had come from India to China to revive the spirit of Buddhism. China at the time was ruled by Emperor Wu of Liang (502-549). The Emperor met the Bodhidharma and said something like the following to him "As Emperor of China I have been a champion of Buddhism, I had funded the translations of the sutras into Chinese, I have established monasteries and I have spread Buddhism throughout China. What merit do I get for these virtuous deeds?" The Bodhidharma answered "You get no merit". What could this possibly mean? If a man who has spread Buddhism to China gets no merit how is it we can expect "mountains of merit" by merely sitting Zazen?

In the Prajna Paramita Heart Sutra we chant the words "No path, no wisdom and no gain". To understand this confusion about merit we must go back to Line 1 of our song. From the beginning all beings are Buddha. That means that everything is perfect as it is. That means that there is no place to go and no time to be there. That means there is no increase or decrease. Further in the same Sutra it tells us that when we walk the path we progress no further and come no nearer. Later in our Song we will hear the words "In going and returning, we never leave home". There is no going and returning. We are always at home in the bosom of Buddha.

The unending blessings are the joys we receive when we commit to follow the Dharma. Our lives become calmer and more focused. We were born to realize our true mind and show our Buddha Nature. These are the blessings and merits of Zazen.

21. And if we turn inward and prove our True Nature,

In his 1967 book on Hakuin's Song in Praise of Zazen, Zenkei Shibayama divided the song into three key parts. Part One, Line 1, From the beginning all beings Are Buddha. The Second part of the Song begins here in Line 21, And if we turn inward and prove our True Nature. The Third Part is the final line, Line 35, This very body, the Body of Buddha. For Shibayama, Line 21 is thus the heart of this song. It tells us what we must do to connect Line 1 with Line 35. Line 1 is an abstract and difficult philosophical claim to understand. How can all beings be Buddha? How can bullies and murderers be Buddha? How can (to quote the famous Koan) a dog have Buddha Nature? How can we say that grass or fish or mosquitos are Buddha? This puzzle can only be solved after we have achieved Kensho or Enlightenment. In other writings, Hakuin says that anyone who is a practitioner of Zen and has not achieved Kensho is a fraud. (I will pass quickly over that comment as it may hit me too close to home!) For Hakuin, Kensho is the whole point of Zazen. Zen Buddhism may be called a religion or a philosophy of life but it is first and foremost a technique of liberation.

Kensho comes from the Japanese root words Ken which means seeing or observing and Sho which means reality. These come from the Ch'an Chinese root words Jian ad Xing which mean to See into the property, quality, or nature of a thing. It is a direct seeing into reality. A pointing to what is before words and language. This is the result of our inward turn. Line 21 gives us the tool to achieve this end.

Inward does not mean to turn away from the world but it does mean we focus on what is right in front of us. Turn off the television news. Put down the paper. Forget the latest movie or soap opera. Look at a flower. Breathe in the air. Taste the tea you have brewed. Smile.

22. That True Self is no-self, our own self is no-self,

The concept of no-self is a hard thing for those of us reared in the Western religious and philosophical traditions. What can it mean to say there is no-self? For me, it means we do not exist as a separate being apart from everything. I am my male hormones. I am the strong tea I drank today that speeded up my mental processes. I am the chemical reactions of the food I had for breakfast. I am the hot or cold of my environment. I react to sunlight or grey rainy days differently. If I had not enough or too much sleep I am different. If my day at work was miserable or disastrous that might impact who I am that night. Think of how mood altering drugs like alcohol, marijuana, opioids, heroin, prozac, or quaaludes can "change" our self. People say "I was not myself last night." This is simply the recognition of the connection of that vague abstract thing we call self to everything around it.

But it is not just the chemicals, hormones, energies, and circumstances of our lives that shift and move the self. Our self is the product of DNA, genetics, and the behavioral forces that shaped us. If you almost drowned as a toddler you may carry a fear of swimming. There are DNA configurations that make many members of a racial group lactose intolerant, or prone to alcoholism, or more likely to succumb to certain illnesses. There are genetic dispositions to certain types of cancer or diabetes. Add to this family or cultural tendencies, those things that are sometimes called stereotypes. Some cultures value education, others value courage, others have different traditions of courtship, marriage, passage to adulthood, and behavior. How often do we see small gestures or habits we have that we copied from our parents or grandparents at an age when we were so young we can't recall where that habit comes from? How much sugar we put in our coffee, if we bite our nails, or if we use profanity might not be a personal choice but a habit we picked up from a parent. What then is our "self"?

For the Buddha any identification with a separate self than ours alone is a mistake. But it is not just any mistake, it is the fundamental mistake that separates us from everything else, isolates us, and puts a wall up between myself and the world. When the Buddha became enlightened he realized that a separate unique self was an illusion. If we see ourselves as separate beings we see ourselves as limited and isolated. But that is not the worst result of this mistake. Seeing ourselves as separate and different from the world, nature, and other people we now have our perception and reality as two different things. We now have me and you, us and them. We have I and it. We now have a dualistic universe where the difference becomes a point of conflict and suffering. If I am different from the world I can say the world should, could, or ought to be different than it is. If I am different from you, you may be my enemy. Dualism opens the door for judgements, discrimination, likes and dislikes.

Buddha, on his enlightenment day, saw the emptiness of all distinctions which revealed instead the connectedness of all things. Once we see we are connected to all things, we see that words like ought, should, not, don't like, like, love, hate, and different all goes away. This flow transforms our experience of time as well. No longer is there past, present, and future but it has been replaced by the eternal now.

23. we go beyond ego and past clever words.

Zen is not an intellectual theory. Zen is, at its heart, not a philosophy. Zen is not in our heads. Zen is a technique of liberation whose aim is a two-step process. First, the practitioner must come to Kensho, Satori, Enlightenment. Second, once Enlightenment has been achieved, the practitioner must translate that wisdom into compassion in an effort to awaken other beings to the truth of reality.

To be enlightened is to drop body and mind. What does this mean? It means that we no longer live inside our limited skin surrounded by our limiting beliefs.   There is no self because there is no single thing disconnected from everything else.   Everything is flowing together like a great river.   The yellow tulip waving in the spring air, the brook flowing past a little bridge, and my eyes following it are all one thing.   This is not something we can make an argument for or give evidence for.   It is the truth of Zen.

It has been my experience that Zen attracts an unusual number of educated and sophisticated practitioners.   I have sat Zazen with surgeons, philosophy professors, psychologists, and even a stray bank president.   These people are educated and often very skilled in argument and intellectual ability.   All of these skills are useless in Zen.   In Zen we just sit and after some time we are (hopefully) released from the machinations of thought.   Cleverness is not what is required here, determination to achieve liberation is what is needed.

24. Then the gate to the oneness of cause-and-effect is thrown open.

Cause and effect are the way we in the West look at all events. Time has a past, present, and future. Effects in the present flow from causes in the past. Effects in the future will flow from causes in the present. In this way of looking at time, there is a now and a not now. But in Kensho we are booted out of time measured by a clock. Once we have achieved enlightenment and the "gate is open" there is no longer past and future. There is only the here and now. Our focus is no longer on the mistakes and regrets of the past or the anxieties or fears of the future. We are no longer steered by ghosts of our past or the demons of our future. We are simply in the here and now without comment. So the gate to cause and effect, the gate to past and present is thrown open and we are only in the present.

The Third Patriarch of the Chinese Chan line, Seng-T'san (496-606 CE) wrote a volume called the Hsin Hsin Ming which can be translated in English as Faith in Mind. In this work he tells us "Do not seek truth, only cease to cherish opinions", "When love and hate are absent, perception becomes clear", and "To set up what you like against what you don't like is the disease of mind". Once we follow this advice we stop making distinctions like cause and effect. We leave all mental constructions behind and simply taste the tea.

25. Not two and not three, straight ahead runs the Way.

Once we are in the here and now we no longer see inside and outside as different. My tears become as natural as rain. My voice is a natural as a clear bell ringing in an empty sky. There is no longer the dualism of me and you, now and then, here and there, like and dislike, good and bad. So it is not two or three. It is the wonderful, connected oneness of the now. We are outside of nature, time, and space. We accept what comes and we are along for the ride. The Way, the path, the Tao is the flow of nature. It is not outside of us or away from us. We are always on the path. Thus we do not need to hesitate. Hesitation is a bad thing in Zen. During Zen training a teacher will often ask a practitioner a question about a Koan. The question might be "What is the sound of one hand clapping?" or "Does a dog have Buddha Nature?" or "What was your original face before your parents were born?"

The teacher does not want the student to hesitate while the wheels of the brain are turning out a clever theory. Instead the teacher wants the student to spontaneously demonstrate their oneness with the question. The student must become the question.

26. Our form now being no-form,

The concept of emptiness is an idea that has been an impediment to many Western students of Zen. No-form is another way of saying all phenomena including our own selves are empty. This does not mean that there is absolutely nothing, for that would be absurd. Daffodils are yellow and not red, snakes do not have four legs, and Paris is not west of London. So there is something, otherwise none of those statements would make sense. What emptiness means is not that we have no properties or qualities but that we have no separate, fixed, or abiding properties or qualities. There is no "thing" inside of me like a boulder that is there and persists throughout all the changes and phases of my life. But rather, my connectedness with all things means that I flow with everything around me.

Thich Nhat Hanh uses the term "Interbeing" which means the essential connectedness of all things. Nothing is separate from everything else. This means we are never disconnected or alone. We are as much a part of nature as a mountain stream or a desert cactus. We are at one with everything and everything interpenetrates and is at one with us. Thich Nhat Hanh gives an example:

"...there is a cloud floating in this piece of paper. Without a cloud, there would be no water; without water, the trees cannot grow; without the trees you cannot make paper. So the cloud is in here. The existence of this page is dependent on the existence of a cloud. Paper and cloud are so close..."

Inside of me is not a simple soul or mind that has a static definition. My connection is to all things. I am a myriad of memories, hopes, fears, regrets, and hopes. I am a flow of emotions, thoughts, perceptions and this flow can either harmonize with the flow of the universe (the Tao, the Way, the Path) or it can fight it. We fight it when we start making distinctions between what we think, want, or believe and what is. Once we stop fighting it and let go, we are free.

27. in going and returning we never leave home.

Once we realize our true nature is Buddha Nature, and Buddha Nature is the absolute truth, we are home. We are home wherever we are, be that a palace, a hovel, a prison cell or a hospital bed. We don't need go to heaven and we don't need to avoid hell. We are on the path. More accurately we are on "the far shore".

In the Alagaddupama Sutta, which is a work about clinging to deluded views, we are given the Buddhist metaphor of the raft. A monk comes to river and does not see a way to cross it. So the monk constructs a raft of timbers and vines and proceeds across the river. When he gets to the other shore what need does he have of the raft? As soon as are enlightened, what need do we have for the instructions for enlightenment? If you know where your home is, do you need directions to find it?

Now comes the most important point. The opening line and the closing line of this song tell us all beings are Buddha and we ourselves are Buddha. So there is no river to cross, no shore to get to, and no need of a raft. But in his enlightenment statement Buddha added "but we are too deluded to see this". Our delusion is the old bamboo bucket which has a reflection of the moon in it. Our ego is the old bamboo bucket. Our ego is the heart of our delusions. Once the bottom drops out we are freed from our limited and deluded perspective. The moon has not come and gone in the bamboo bucket. The moon only appeared in the bamboo bucket because the bucket was full of water, just as we are full of opinions, discriminations, and theories. Once we drop our discriminations we are empty and free. Because all beings are Buddha, there is no coming and going, no past or future, only the sacred and shimmering here and now. We are all on the other shore, we just don't know it, like the child of rich birth wandering poor on the earth.

28. Our thought now being no-thought,

It is impossible to stop thinking. Try as we may, thoughts pop up, memories arise, tasks are recalled and right in the middle of meditation we might think we left the oven on back at home. No thought therefore cannot mean to stop thinking. We have mentioned before there are two truths in Buddhism, the absolute and the relative. In relative terms we cannot have no thought. We are machines that are constantly generating thoughts. In Zen we speak of the "monkey mind", a mind that is restless, gossiping, jumping from subject to subject. The monkey is looking for a vine or a tree limb to cling to.

From an absolute point of view we don't need to stop thinking we only need to stop clinging to opinions or ideas. Having a thought is natural, clinging to it is un-Zen. Once we are liberated from making judgments and discrimination we can sit and watch our thoughts go by like we watch the clouds float by on a summer's day. Once we give up our attachment to being right we are free to just look. It will then occur to the Zen practitioner to ask the next logical question; "who is looking"? In this state of not knowing, not attaching, and not fighting we are simply reflecting what we see almost without comment.

29. our dancing and songs are the Voice of the Dharma.

If all beings are Buddha, as we learned in Line 1, then all utterances are the utterances of the Buddha. Once our practice wakes us up from our delusions we realize our essential or real nature. A potter can use clay to make mugs, plates, statutes, bowls, and vases. But the essence of all of those different things is the clay. Our voice is the voice of the Dharma or the teaching. Once we have achieved enlightenment, our dancing and singing truly are the voice of the Dharma. We can then use our dancing and songs to spread the teachings. We recall that a Bodhisattva has forsaken salvation so that they can return to the world and assist other beings in their quest for freedom.

30. How vast is the heaven of boundless Samadhi!

Once enlightenment has freed us from our limited perspective we are part of the unlimited. Our Samadhi, or power of concentration, opens up and connects us with the universe. Boundless Samadhi is heaven because no matter what we experience, good or bad, pleasurable or painful, we are open to it. The word "heaven" here is the right word because when we are in Samadhi we see all beings as Buddha and we see ourselves as part of the flow of being.

31. How bright and transparent the moonlight of wisdom!

There is Zen story that has become a koan or teaching tool to illustrate this point. The nun Chiyono was a student of Bukko of Engaku. For many years Chiyono sat in meditation without achieving enlightenment. Then one night Chiyono was out carrying water back to the monastery. As she carried the water she noticed that the full moon was reflected in the water she was carrying. Suddenly the bottom of the pail broke and as the water rushed out the image of the moon went with it. At this moment

Chiyono experienced Kensho or sudden enlightenment. Chiyono composed a poem to celebrate the occasion.

I did my best to save the old bucket

But the bamboo was weak

At last the bottom dropped away

No more water in bucket

No more moon in water

The water in the bucket is our limited consciousness. The moon that is reflected in the water is Buddha Nature. Buddha Nature can be reflected in a million buckets of water without losing its light. This story in the intersection between absolute truth (Buddha Nature) and relative truth (I seem to be a unique person existing in real time and space). Once I drop body and mind there is no more dualism, no more conflict, no bucket, no water, and no moon.

32. What is there outside us? What is there we lack?

If all beings are Buddha, we lack nothing. If all beings are Buddha, there is nothing outside of us. If all beings are Buddha, there is no place to come and go from. This is the absolute or ultimate truth. At the same time we live in the realm of sensory phenomenon and it seems that there are things we lack. The fundamental delusion is that there is anything that is not already Buddha and that includes us. We need not seek anymore because we have arrived.

33. Nirvana is openly shown to our eyes.

Nirvana is a Sanskrit term for the Pali term Nibbana which literally means to "blow out" like blowing out a candle. Nirvana is the goal of all Buddhist practice. In some Buddhist tradition the word Nirvana is used in a way that is similar to the Christian concept of Heaven. In our Zen tradition the word Nirvana means "release" which means that while we stay in this world we are released from the pains and struggles that our ego experiences when we struggle against the world. We have discussed the three poisons; Greed, Anger, and Ignorance. Nirvana is the blowing out, or extinguishing, of these three poisons. When we become enlightened and experience Kensho with a thunder flash we see the delusions fostered by the three poisons. Once I realize that I am Buddha then there is nothing that I truly lack and I should not be greedy. Once I realize all other beings are Buddha doing the best that they can, I am no longer angry at them or wishing them to be anything other than what they are. When I realize all beings are Buddha then I am no longer ignorant. Liberation from the three poisons means that we are no longer living in anger and fear. Once we see the common Buddha nature all being shared we also see that there are no solid and unchanging individual essences that hold us apart. This is the realization of the emptiness of all beings.

Here were are told that Nirvana is openly shown to our eyes. It is not some future time or place where we go to when we die. Nirvana is openly shown to our eyes right here at this moment.

34. This land where we stand is the Pure Lotus Land

If Nirvana is here and now we are presently, at this moment, in the Pure Lotus Land but we are too deluded to see it. The Pure Land in Buddhism is where the Bodhisattva dwells. It is a place free from the suffering attachments bring. In the pure land there are still thoughts, perceptions, memories and insights but the Bodhisattva does not cling them. When we realize that we already in the Pure Lotus Land there is no reason for Greed, Anger and Ignorance. When we realize we are in the Pure Lotus Land there is no desire to be anywhere else.

Nagarjuna writes that Samsara and Nirvana are one in the same. But if Samsara is suffering and Nirvana is bliss how can this be true? Is not suffering an obstacle to bliss? But Nagarjuna prepares us for this claim by showing that all individual existing things are empty and insubstantial. Thus, this life of mine, with its ups and downs, my aches and pains, my joys and sorrows is the manifestation of the Buddha. The Lotus flower has its roots in the mud. The roots go down deep in the mud and slime and from that dirty dark place blooms, on the surface of the pond, a flower of immense beauty. Without suffering we would not learn.

35. And this very body, the body of Buddha.

Line 35 is the payoff of the whole Song in Praise of Zazen. All beings are Buddha is an abstract and theoretical claim. But Line 35 say THIS body, my body, me right here and right now is Buddha. Me with all of my imperfections, addictions, bad habits, shameful failures, polluted desires…..I am Buddha. There is nowhere else I need to go and nothing else I need to do. I am the Buddha. But I take this one step further. I am a Bodhisattva. Which means I am striving to be awakened so that I might assist other sentient beings in their own evolution towards enlightenment.   What   wondrous   news.

PART III-THE STRUCTURE OF THE SONG

In his excellent 1967 book On Zazen Wasan that is long out of print, Zen Mater Zenkei Shibayama, Abbot of the Nanzenji Monastery in Kyoto, divided The Song in Praise of Zazen into forty-four lines and three parts.   His translation differs slightly from the one used in this text. He laid out the structure in the following way.

Part one is line one which he called The Introduction: "All beings are Buddha".

Part two he calls the Main Text is line thirty "And testify to the truth of self nature".

Part Three he calls The Conclusion is line thirty-five "Your person, the body of Buddha".

While his analysis is excellent and was a great benefit in the writing of this work, I wanted to dig a little deeper in showing how one section leads to another and how one line supports the one that preceded or follows. To accomplish this I have divided Hakuin's Song of Zazen into ten elements or sections. You will find a schemata of this at the end of this section. In PART TWO of this work we have already analyzed the elements one by one. You will see there is beautiful logic and flow to the ten elements. I agree with Abbot Shibayama in that the First Line, All beings are Buddha, and the Last Line, This very body, the body of Buddha are variations on the same idea. Let us here restate the three sections that Abbot Shibayama has suggested.

Section One tells us that ALL beings are Buddha.

Section Two tells us we don't know that we are Buddha. It tells us we are not yet fully conscious of the claim made in Section One.

Section Three then tells us how we can find out if this is true.

My reconstruction breaks the song into ten smaller parts to better illustrate their flow and connection.

Hakuin's Song of Zazen .

Part I Our Essential Nature is Buddha Nature.

Claim made in the first line and the last line (1-35)

1. From the beginning all beings are Buddha.

The claim that All Beings are Buddha is expounded upon by an analogy

2. Like water and ice, without water no ice,

3. outside us no Buddhas.

Part II Why Don't We See This? Because We Have Looked In The Wrong Place.

4. How near the truth, yet how far we seek.

This statement is unpacked using two analogies

Analogy 1.

5. Like one in water crying, "I thirst!"

Analogy 2

6. Like a child of rich birth wand'ring poor on

7. this earth we endlessly circle the six worlds.

Part III. Why Have We Not Seen The Truth? Because We Are Deluded.

Claim:

8. The cause of our sorrow is ego delusion.

Analogy to Support Claim.

9. From dark path to dark path we've wandered in darkness,

Part IV How can we realize our Buddha Nature? Zazen Is The Path

10. How can we be freed from birth and death?

11. The gateway to freedom is zazen Samadhi;

12. Beyond exaltation, beyond all our praises, the pure Mahayana.

Part V. How must we live in order to realize our Buddha nature?

13. Observing the Precepts, Repentance and Giving,

14. the countless good deeds and the way of right living, all come from zazen.

15. Thus one true samadhi extinguishes evils. It purifies karma, dissolving obstructions.

Part VI. If we live this life what can we hope to gain?

16. Then where are the dark paths to lead us astray?

17. The Pure Lotus Land is not far away.

18. Hearing this truth, heart humble and grateful.

19. To praise and embrace it, to practice its wisdom

20. brings unending blessings. bring mountains of merit.

Part VII. When we do Zazen we will see our true selves and our true selves are empty

21. And if we turn inward and prove our True Nature, that

22. True Self is no-self, our own self is no-self,

23. we go beyond ego and past clever words.

Part VIII. After seeing emptiness inside and can we see emptiness outside?

24. Then the gate to the oneness of cause-and-effect is thrown open.

25. Not two and not three, straight ahead runs the Way.

Part IX Once we see emptiness we are liberated.

26. Our form now being no-form,

27. in going and returning we never leave home.

28. Our thought now being no-thought,

Part X. This brings joy and freedom when it is realized.

29. our dancing and songs are the Voice of the Dharma.

30. How vast is the heaven of boundless Samadhi!

31. How bright and transparent the moonlight of wisdom!

Part XI. We then stop searching because we have found The answer.

32. What is there outside us? What is there we lack?

33. Nirvana is openly shown to our eyes.

34. This land where we stand is the Pure Lotus Land

Part X. We restate The first line but make it personal

35. And this very body, the body of Buddha.

The first line (which is echoed in the last line) tells us all beings are Buddha. This point is illustrated by three analogies. This gives rise to a question in line 8. If all beings are Buddha why don't we know this? This question is answered in line 10 when we see how we can know this. Once we know this, we find out in line 13 that we must begin to live differently. If we have this realization and live according the dharma, line 16 shows us what we will gain. Once we have looked inward and thus seen our true nature we see it as empty (line 21) we no longer grasp or fight. Once we see the emptiness inside we can look and see the emptiness outside in line 24. Once that is accomplished we are liberated and free as we see in line 26. This brings joy and freedom as we learn in line 29. In line 32 we have stopped searching. Line 35, the final line, restates the first line and tells us we now know that abstract claim made in line 1.

Conclusion- A Personal Reflection

My fervent hope is that this little work has either introduced you to a wonderful chant or reawakened your thinking about it. For the last year and half, my personal practice has not been focused on solving koans or watching my breath. Instead I have recited the Song in Praise of Zazen over and over all throughout my day. As stated at the outset, I believe this short chant contains the whole wisdom of Buddhism in a compact and understandable form. Just as a poem can sometimes say more than a novel, this chant is one gateway to seeing the world as it is. After a lifetime as a teacher of philosophy and religion I have found all I need to know in these 35 lines and 295 words. There are many schools of Buddhism and countless interpretations of the Dharma. This chant is the heart of all of those teachings. For me, the Song in Praise of Zazen shows us we are already in Nirvana and walking barefoot in the Pure Lotus Land. Just breathe and everything else will take care of itself.

Glossary

Buddha: This term has several meanings. It can means the founder of Buddhism but it can also mean the essential nature of all things. Buddha nature is free, enlightened and compassionate. This is the state we seek when we sit Zazen.

Bodhidharma: This is the founder of Chinese Chan Buddhism which was the precursor to Zen. He was in the lineage of the Buddha but left India to bring the Dharma to China.

Bodhisattva: One who aims at enlightenment by practicing meditation and compassion. The Bodhisattva seeks the ent not just of him or herself but freeing all beings from the suffering that results from delusion.

Dharma: The teachings of the Buddha

Dukka: The suffering that results from the loss of something, person or idea that we once held dear. Anything that brings us pleasure by its possession can bring us suffering by its loss. Zen aims to minimize or ideally eliminate suffering.

Enlightenment: The realization that clinging to things that are impermanent will not make us happy or give us peace. The detachment of our emotions from things that fade away and focusing instead upon the present moment in all of its reality.

Hell: In Buddhism we are not sent to Hell by a vengeful God. We make choices that create our own unhappiness and suffering. Heaven and Hell are destinations in this world we end up in by our choices and our acceptance of things we cannot change.

Hungry Ghosts: In the Buddhist stories there are spirits with small mouths and huge stomachs. This means they can not get enough food in their small mouth to satisfy their hunger. This is metaphor for the desires such as gluttony, hoarding of money or goods, alcoholism and other vices where we cannot satisfy the urge that compels us on.

Jukai: Ceremony where we accept the Buddhist Precepts and commit to following the Dharma.e

Kensho: The Japanese word for Enlightenment.

Koan: Linguistic traps or puzzles that are used to free the mind form logical habits and help us open our eyes and see clearly.

Lotus Land: A term in Buddhism for a world without corruption, pain or suffering. We are told in our song that this land where stand is the Pure Lotus Land. While this seems paradoxical it means that if we open our eyes we will see we have already reached our destination.

Mahayana: This refers to the path of the Bodhisattva who seeks the release of all beings.

Nirvana: In early Buddhism Nirvana was thought of as kind of heaven we can go to where we will no longer suffer. In Zen we think of it as living in this world with our eyes open and seeing things as they truly are. The promise of Zen is a kind of heaven on earth if we can wake up.

Prajna Paramita: The wisdom contained in the teachings of Buddha.

Precepts: The ethical rules we should follow to help us achieve enlightenment

Rinzi: A school of Zen that emphasises the practice and discipline needed to attain Enlightenment. Koans are often used to help the student open their mind.

Rohatsu: The day of Buddha's Enlightenment celebrated on December 8th.

Samadhi: The power we gain by sitting in Zazen. As we sit, our energy settles and hopefully our delusions will drop away allowing us to wake up.

Samsara: The world for suffering.

Sangha: A community of practitioners, monks, nuns or lay persons, who sit together in Zazen and listen to the Dharma together.

Shunyata: Sanskrit word sometimes translated as emptiness. A better way of thinking about this is that all beings undergo changes and this means that what they are is not something eternal undergoes transition. There is no substance that is eternal and unchanging like the concept of the soul in Christianity.

Soto: A school of Zen that emphasizes our Buddha Nature as soon as we sit in Zazen

Sutra: A work containing the teachings of the Buddha.

Taoism: A school of Chinese thought founded by Lao Tzu emphasizing the harmony of human beings and nature. Tao means the path and we are urged to return to simplicity and pay attention to what is near at hand.

Unsoi: The name given to new monks in a Zen monastery. It means "cloud water".

Wu-Wei: The Taoist concept of non-doing. It means we should not try to control things but harmonize with them. By doing this we can do little but much can be accomplished.

Zazen: Sitting meditation

Zen: Please return to page one.

SELECT BIBLIOGRAPHY

Addiss, Stephen, ed. *Zen Sourcebook: Traditional Documents from China, Korea, and Japan.* Hackett Publications, 2008.

Aitken, Robert, *Taking the Path of Zen*, North Point Press, 1982.

Ch'en, Kenneth, *Buddhism in China: A Historical Survey*, Princeton University Press, 1972.

Cleary, Thomas, *The Original Face: An Anthology of Rinzai Zen.* Grove Press, 1978.

Fields, Rick. *How the Swans Came to the Lake: A Narrative History of Buddhism in America,* Shambhala Press, 1992.

Fisher, Norman, and Moon, Susan, What is Zen? Plain Talk for a Beginners Mind, Shambhala Press, 2016

Gregory, Peter, ed., *Sudden and Gradual: Approaches to Enlightenment in Chinese Thought*, University of Hawaii Press, 1987.

Heine, Steven, *Opening a Mountain: Koans of the Zen Masters*, Oxford University Press, 2002.

Heine, Steven and Dale S. Wright, eds., *The Koan: Texts and Contexts in Zen Buddhism*, Oxford University Press, 2000.

Heine Steven and Wright, Dale, eds. *The Zen Canon: Understanding the Classic Texts*. New York: Oxford University Press, 2004.

Loori, John Daido, *Mountain Record of Zen Talks*, Shambhala Press, 2008.

Lowe, Albert, *Hakuin's Chant in Praise of Zazen with Commentary*, Amazon Digital Services, 2017.

Shibayama, Zenkei, *On Zazen Wasan, Hakuin's Song of Zazen,* Kyoto Press, 1967.

Suzuki, D.T., *Manual of Zen Buddhism,* FQ Classics Press, 1935.

Suzuki, Shunryu, *Zen Mind, Beginner's Mind.* New York: Weatherhill, 1970.

Kazuaki Tanahashi, Kaim, ed. *Beyond Thinking: A Guide to Zen Meditation* (by Zen Master Dogen). Boston: Shambhala Publications, 2004

Waddell, Norman, trans., *The Essential Teachings of Zen Master Hakuin,* Shambhala Publications, Inc., 1994

Waddell, Norman Zen *Words for the Heart: Hakuin's Commentary on the Heart Sutra,* Boston, Shambhala Press, 1996

Waddell, Norman, *The Complete Poison Blossoms from a Thicket of Thorn: The Zen Records of Hakuin Ekaku*, Berkley, Counterpoint Press, 2017

van de Wetering, Janwillem, *The Empty Mirror*. New York, Pocket Books, 1972.

Wu, Jiang *Enlightenment in Dispute: The Reinvention of Chan Buddhism in Seventeenth-Century China*. New York: Oxford University Press, 2008.

Yampolsky, Philip, *The Zen Master Hakuin: Selected Writings*. New York: Columbia University Press, 1971.

Yampolsky, Philip, *The Platform Sutra of the Sixth Patriarch*, Columbia University Press, 1978.

Hakuin's Song in Praise of Zazen

Dr. Frank McCluskey

Made in the USA
Coppell, TX
12 September 2022

83011343R00075